THE WORLD'S GONE
MAD . . . HASN'T IT?

THE WORLD'S GONE MAD . . . HASN'T IT?

POEMS FROM A FRUSTRATED REVOLUTIONARY

Richard James Allen

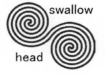

Swallowhead Publishing 2010

SWALLOWHEAD PUBLISHING
3 The Green, Calne, Wiltshire, SN11 8DG
www.swallowhead.co.uk
info@swallowhead.co.uk

British Library Cataloguing in Publication Data.
A catalogue record for this book is available
from the British Library

ISBN: 978-0-9564844-0-6

Design and Typeset by
Jim and Peggy Grich at *eBookProducers*
All Photography by the Author

Printed and bound by Lightning Source UK Ltd, Chapter House, Pitfield, Kiln Farm, Milton Keynes, MK11 3LW

CONTENTS

Preface

The twin towers of Democracy and Capitalism have fallen, and a dictatorial "New World Order" is here. In the eighties it seemed we faced global destruction from nuclear war, now we also have "terrorism", peak oil and global warming to occupy our thoughts. We are indeed living in interesting times.

I was born in 1966 and this locates me in a group sometimes referred to as the "Blank Generation". This collection of poems is my personal record of the emotions of living through these times. The poems are unflinching in their truth to my experiences, and I am sure readers will identify with both the hope and desperation presented here. My survival mechanism is often black caustic humour, which I hope will provide plenty of entertainment, as well as food for thought.

I was first inspired to write poetry in 1990 whilst a passenger aboard a small open boat on Lake Titicaca. The Lake is nearly 4000 metres above sea level and the altitude causes distortion of one's perception of distance. For hours and hours, ten of us sailed in the direction of what seemed to be a small nearby island, and yet it never seemed to get any closer. The air was thin, I was chewing coco leaves, and the Indian crew onboard the boat were silent and meditative. I entered a state of altered consciousness. I happened to have a pen and a piece of paper with me, so I took them out and started to write.

My poems have been well received at readings and poetry slams, so about a year ago I decided I would like to share them with a wider audience. Originally conceived as editing down to a single volume, the final result is a pair of books which read like Yin/Yang, Heaven/Hell companions. This book (Yang/Hell), which is the first of the two, is divided into four parts, which also aids an allegorical interpretation.

My thanks go out to everyone who has helped with the production of this book: Alda, Mum and Dad; all the friends who helped with proof reading and editing; the typesetters, designers and printers; everyone who has ever encouraged me or supported me in any way and the anonymous graffiti artists, some of whose images appear in this book.

I am an artist
I have the key
I hope one day it will flow from me
The sweetest verse
The sublimest rhyme
Poems to stand the test of time

Part I

I Exist

There's an Artist in the bakers
He's living among us
There's an Artist in the street
She's living among us
There are Artists on the bus
They're living among us
There's Art among us now
It's living within us

I Want to Point in Every Direction

I want to point in every direction
Like the thing at the end of the pier
That 10p contraption

I don't want to miss out or shut my mind down
I want to shout out and rhyme
Flowers or puns
I want to walk
Fly
Run

I've seen a million colours come out to greet my eyes
I know they're always there
To lift me
To inspire

But don't get me wrong
I'm not talking about the physically gifted bowling along
I'm talking about a feeling
A dreaming
A seeming
A rightness
A lightness
A shimmering life
Beaming with brightness

3   *Richard Allen*

Oh airy fairy words slipping in my ears
Like shampoo bubble worlds
But don't be like that
Don't pull down your hat
Don't be a fool
Don't be rude
Because I'm talking about you

And me

Night-Watch

Walking empty corridors
Patrolling the silent building while the whole
world sleeps
The planet breaths out
Takes stock
Goes deep
Invader!
Searching the giant kitchen for treats
Illegal underworld
Burglar's playground
Only (my) shadows I meet

It's the other side of the coin
Watching
Listening
Sixth sense prickling
Distant car whooshing
Reality too far to rescue me from fantasy

I am sat apart
Special
Like the first man in space
Just sat in a room
But because of the hour
Because of the moon
I am a pioneer
Privileged
I am the night-watch

Richard Allen

Late

A single white cloud sits atop a single green tree
A white rag dances on the end of a ladder
A flag's crisp shadow falls randomly on the warm
Bath stone
And the sun glints in the scarlet paintwork of a
new car

I am late
But a second sun signaling from distant woodland
Tells me that on a paradise morning such as this
Time is not important

I surrender to my tardiness

Autumn Thought

On seeing the orange band of autumn trees
The emotional focus turning in my mind's eye
adjusts to softness

Childhood country walks
A witch's hat roundabout
Conkers and a musty dead leaf smell
The outdoors
Mum and Dad and Brother Pete
Granddad
Grandma
Princes and kings
Fresh
Light
Happy

Where might I find the vividness of this evocation?
The answer is in every second
Every breath and every footfall
Until the day I die

I am trying not to be sentimental
My rational mind has no place for sentimentality
Logic tries to corral these memories
Yet a soft filter constantly descends to deny me
the moral high ground

Sitting in the Same Place

How long could I sit in the same place?

Outside?
Summer?
Warm pavement?
Or winter?
Covered in ice?

Inside?
Well forever
In theory at least
But I might want to straighten my legs now and
then
Or when bored shout like a beast

A prisoner I'd be
A protester sitting in a tree
A Buddhist dressed in orange
Motionless and waiting for a gong
Begging
Two pairs of trousers and leggings
Homeless
Staring
Life nearly gone

Hospitalised
Sound heightened
Senses sensitised

Perhaps being still will humble me
Make me realise

*A Very Confused Individual

Too much time has been wasted getting things
perfect
Now what's left is verging on tragic
Having spent so long making a little really count
The time has come
The realization arrived at
That what is needed can just be taken
Rules are there to flout

Music cannot be made on your own
In your house in your home
It is out in the cities
Out in the mountains

How movement is made comes from a love
How decisions are made should be the result of
touching the earth
Touching the everything
And making the effort to reach for above

So where next is there to turn for a very confused
individual?
Soothing waters of musical answers
Please don't present a habit of craziness
Show mercy
Show a melody to live by) Oasis
Help avoid a starving tear-stained mess) uncle
Jon
Peace for all in their own way
Smooth running to stay
Syndrome

Richard Allen

Poet Soul

Poet soul
Impractical
Swept along by the inertia of moment to
moment need
Trodden under circumstance
Winning by accident
God's gift or karma
Deserving of love

Poet soul
Untidy
Disorganised
Late
Charming
Shrouded in the luck you choose to wear
People come to help you shoulder the weight of
the impossibility of your life
And the unlikelihood of your existence

Yeah !, Yes .

Mixed media self portrait by the author (original in colour)

Can You Hear The Calling?

This poem may flow from a hesitant pen
Or it may not
It may start
Flow
Stop

Fragile insect bounce upon the page
Bumble round weary eyes
Glint in the candle light
Clockwork mind

So peaceful a night that a hiss descends
Another timeless hour
Marked by tons of solid
Ancient
Discordant metal
Throbbing
Pulsating hiss

From that uneasy peace
Imagined real horrors rise
Frightening in that now no tears fall from my
eyes
Even though the suffering is also mine

How many more taste this awareness?
How many more couldn't care less?
How many more have their own sort of stress?
How many more would like to redress...?

Now my pen's writing smaller
Like a body shrinking from being taller
Yet still they are falling
Can you hear the calling?

Seaside Dream

Blinded by the sun
Winter dogman gone
Fruit days coming along
Woman's gaze
Floating and wrong

Returned by me now
Lost season somehow
Jewels at my feet
Hoping sweetness I'll reap
Symbols I fear
Carried away in the air

Time turning Tide
What is there to find?
Stunted by my pride
That is why I lied

More still will come to witness the fun
It comes dressed as a man for History's grand
plan
Another wave turns and flies with the birds

I was told where I am is the place it can be
So why am I looking for things I can't see?
Why am I searching for a heart that is free?

Lying in Bed

Preparing the ground
Dusting my broom
Waiting for the wave that's going to take me
someplace

Everything's in order
The calm before the storm
Hoping you'll be with me
I hope it's not a dream

Looking at the detail
Always sorting sticks
Waiting for the moment that'll make me alive

Another cup of tea
A little lie down
Another half hour
And I'll get out of my dressing gown

I'm having a lie in
I've hit the snooze button yet again
Today's revolution's in the bin
Tomorrow I'll rouse my friends

Lying in bed with the world in my hands
Lying in bed with the world in my head

Richard Allen

What Will the Tide Wash Up?

What will the tide wash up?
Will it bring you joy or will it force your tears?
Or something in between?
A decision to be made?

Will it bring you riches?
Will it bear bad news?
Or something in between?
A bold gamble or indecisive fade?

It is possible for anything to be left behind (for you)
When the sea has gone home

So let's go down to the shore
Let's meet our destiny
Let's take our awareness
And let's go right now

What will the tide wash up?
Will it bring a woman?
Will it bring a man?
Or will it pose a riddle
That is waiting to be solved?

The Illusion Life Weaves

The Illusion life weaves is dissolved by a thought
What really goes on is never-ending and free
I try not to carry life's baggage with quite such a sigh
For as death grows nearer
I might not know why

Man Knows Nothing (For Flordemayo)

We know how to fly
We know how to read and write
We know how to compute
We know how to make and play the lute
We know nothing
Man knows nothing

We know how to split the atom
We know how to remove genes from an apple
We know how to train dogs
We know God
We know nothing
Man knows nothing

We know chaos
We know the weather
We know quantum physics
We know about the paranormal and mystics
We know nothing
Man knows nothing

We know about ghosts
We know how three thousand tonne boats float
We know how to make money
We know how to be funny
We know nothing
Man knows nothing

We know how to walk on the moon
We know the mating call of a female racoon
We know how to give people organ swaps
We know how to feed the world with crops
We know nothing
Man knows nothing

We know why the dinosaurs fell
We know about heaven and hell
We know about gravity's pull
We know it all
We know nothing
(Man knows nothing)

Richard Allen

We Are Nature

We just wade in with our eyes shut
Ignorant of our toxic aura
Killing just by living
Our breathing naturally causes deep human
sadness
Wounded nature grieves unsentimentally
It flies to the next nest
Repeats its cycle
We are nature

Embrace

Just as the last leaf of autumn flutters from the
now naked tree
Just as the first grey hair appears on a human
head
Change
The persistence of time will always be present

So live as you always mean to
Before the first wrinkle appears at your eye
Love as you always intend to
Before your skin hangs loose
Turns grey and dies

Embrace all things before they pass

Life Is the Supreme Triumph

Life is the supreme triumph
Life is the ultimate disaster
You choose which
But you had better be quick
Before it slips away
Wriggles out of your grasp
Before it changes its skin

Mixed media self portrait by the author (original in colour)

Sanpaku

They say that it's a sign
You've invited a new guest
That guest is your own shadow
Sitting by your soul inside your chest

Be they blue or brown
There might be two moons rising
Sanpaku is coming for you
There is no use in hiding

Slipping from the fat and felt
Rolling off the ball
Bone and smoke and feathers
Will not break your fall

When there's death around the eyes
There will be two moons rising

Chased by reality
Followed out of the forest
Pursued by destiny
Disturbed in your night-time refuge

Be they green or blue
There might be two moons rising
Sanpaku is coming for you
There is no use in hiding

Sanpaku won't choose a fool
Just as it won't choose the wise
It sits behind your eyeballs
Asking two moons to rise

Wrong and Right

Down is up
Right is left
Peace is war
And life is death

Part II

I Experience

Life is not lived among sight, sound, smell,
taste and touch
It is lived in a single "sense" that is everything
This single "thing" is the emotion of experiencing
the above five senses, and will override all else
when life is being lived in a truly inspiring way

Poem of the Day

Leek and Potato

Richard Allen

Blokey Geezer

Punch me softly on the cheek
When you're with me up the boozer
'Cause I'm your proper mate
I'm a fuckin' blokey geezer

I can down my pints
Hold my own in fights
I smell like Nike
But have national pride

Without my shirt tucked in
I join the sea of youth
Becoming just like all the rest
In blotting out the truth

I'm living all the "man" clichés
Beer promotion free shades
I'm thirty-something but bloody cool
'Cause I can still win at pool

Sometimes I just don't add up
Somehow things just ain't quite right
Something in me's gonna pop
Somewhere there's an ego stopped

Skinhead

Skinhead 'till the day of death
Skinhead 'till the dying breath
Oxblood Marten's
Fred Perry or Sherman
Pride in wearing a uniform

This is the neighbourhood
Shoulder to shoulder where the crew once stood
Grew up together
Know these streets well
Spilled blood together
Inked skin together

Patriarch
Patriot
Greying head held high
Belonging
Loyal
Bulldog guy

Strong identity
No need to think
Beneath the skin does the ego shrink?
Without a badge
Without a place

How much home do we need?
How alone?
Do we live only to feed?
Free of friends
Free of greed

Skinhead
City cat with bowler hat
Skinhead
Farmer
Woolies
Wellies
Quad-bike
Tractor and that

Bury me a Brit
A Nazi or a Jew
Is there a need for football as much as for food?
Is there a need for real ale round the table
In the local with mates?
Is there a need for murder and hate?

Home
Working class
A toff
Peace march in a pint glass
Froth
A laugh
Telly
Family
And at last
Home

They're Different That's All

I stepped out in the sunshine and found myself a
long long way from home

Their eyes followed me as I went past
Mistrust flashed its way up and down the street
I thought this wouldn't happen back in England
As I was stoned with looks from head to feet

The harshness in their ruddy butcher's faces
was only mine turned inside out
This wouldn't happen back in blighty
Outraged we'd scream and shout

They're different that's all

It's all about politeness
Customs when we're feeding
Manners while we're getting fat
Smiling while we're cheating

So what am I doing up on my high horse?
What colour is my honour?
No colour of course
What flag is wrapped around decency?
How long can reputation last?
For better or worse
I am British to my dying gasp

I've Been Round Pete Doherty's House

I might be a talker
But I'm certainly not a stalker
I'm not a blogger or a blagger
I'm not a fag
A nag or on skag
I'm not your Dad

I'm not a journalist
Or stylist
Or racist
You're not on a hate list

I'm not a film-maker
Or marriage breaker
I'm not star-struck or fucked up
I'm not on the make
It's not about
Take
Take
Take

I'm not even a fan
So why should I land
At your door with guitar in hand
Last Monday
Wanting a jam?

Dream Poem

We sat inside and waited patiently.
Then stood outside and waited without knowing we
were waiting.
There was me, the pirate, the thin blond couple, and
surprisingly an occasional, partial cross-dresser.

I was all dressed up, dark suit, thin tie and trilby hat.
You would never have let me wear trousers tucked in
socks and grubby trainers like that.
So I was cool that you were still not by my side as
the guests arrived.
I had no appetite for exotic party food when the first
neatly wrapped sweeties dropped into my palm.
It was unexpected and very very generous.
(They would have kept me up all night)
I placed the potent little parcels in a large round
bowl, in the middle of a small high round table.
All the others (reluctantly generous) followed my
lead until the bowl was filled up.

I climbed the stairs, I slept, and then I returned.

Richard Allen

A plain looking Slavic girl with a beautiful, poetic name and a love for food found on Mexican trains, told me to revisit the scene.
Fill a jug with fruit juice and bring it back from those realms;
Then the entire world will unfold, as this holds the key to all that we need.

Oh, a Cold Summer

Did the dancing girls arrive?
Did the music come alive?
Did the old hippies get stoned?
Did pilled up kids gurn?
Did rhyming couplets couple?
Did a stud's belt unbuckle?
Was Glastonbury a trip?
Or just a pile of shit?

I Want to Care

I can
I can't
I will
I won't
I'm brave
I'm scared
I'm in control
I'm not in control
It matters
It doesn't matter
I love and feel loved
I'm lonely
I'm proud
I'm humiliated

We all care
Who really gives a fuck?
Keep quiet!

Run

Starting out gently
No rhythm yet
No puff
No strain
No sweat

Driving on
Concentrating
Blinkered
Intoxicated

Sweaty
Weak
Done
Hardly fun
But I went on

Out on a run

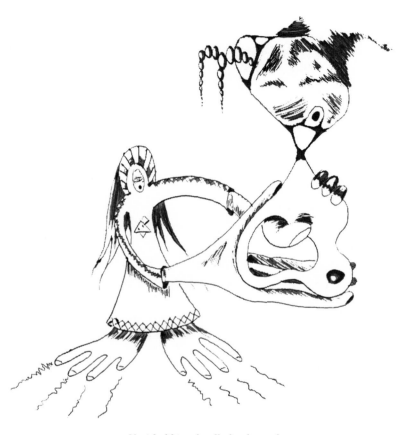

Untitled biro doodle by the author

Happy Birthday Part 1

Happy Birthday Alda

Forty four winters have thawed
Past hundreds of moons
Forty three summers
Forty four soon

It's many more than many
So each year's a golden penny
Every year a priceless gift
More than a thousand men could lift

What's more you love the earth
So she will love you back
With peace on earth and a long life too
And maybe another seven hundred moons

This special day's for you
So make a magic wish
And I will also pray
That all your dreams come true

Happy Birthday Part 2

There's another notch on your wisdom stick
And age my love cannot be tricked
But a clever old world takes care of this
Because for every year more that we're around
Potential for joy is freed
Unbound

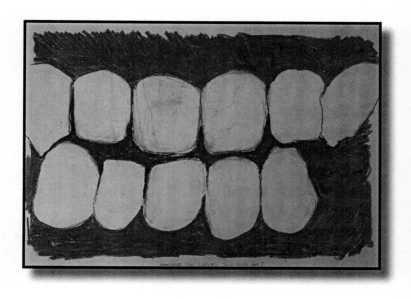

Untitled charcoal drawing by the author

Rik's Rap

I'm sat in the hot seat
I'm going cold turkey
A strict vegetarian
Wanting beef jerky
I know I'm not hip
If I hop on a bus
To the shops
To buy hops
To drown my sox
In alcopops
So God help my soul
If my life's a flop
I wanna come up for air
But won't cut my hair
Wanna ease up the pressure
But don't wanna stress her
I wanna relax
Take my foot off the gas
Don't wanna be brash
Take the cash
I just wanna stop
Avoid the dock
So my life don't go pop

Swindon Chips

A sadness is glimpsed when I eat salty anaemic
chips
Which have been defecated upon
The defecation
A lurid
Red
Sweet ketchup GM contamination

A sense of loss
A helplessness which I don't want to be part of
comes flooding into my consciousness
A winning formula is discussed
In this chip fat
Rank
Funk
Cheap car industrial estate seat

My mind turns to loved ones
Michelle first
Who is condemned in my presence to a wasted
life
Unless I suddenly start to widen my ambition
To encompass risk

Accident

Distant cry of seagulls
Children's playful shrieks
Peaceful whoosh of waves
Recumbent in my coffin
Before I'm sent unto my grave

Eyes and mouth wide open
Held paralysed by sand
Soft and silent terror
The only life left in me
The movement in a finger on one hand

Overwhelmed yet calm
Dreaminess without air
Drugged as nature's way
So I allow life's thieves to come
And carry my young body on

Giant's hands around my bones
Then fingers in my mouth
Breath and sand and coughing
Tears come fast and furious
As show for those I'm loving

Carried to saltwater
Violently revived
Tonnes of sand removed from eyes
Since that day nothing's said
But I came back different no lie

Part III

I Suffer

Suck, Fuck, Shit, Piss, Bleed, Lie and Die!

The World's Gone Mad . . . Hasn't It?

The worlds gone mad hasn't it?
The authorities
The media
The internet
We're scared of ourselves

Tell me how to live my life
Take my money
Take my home
Take my wife
I'll do anything you say
I've got no mind of my own

When you lie to me
I'll say yeah
I'll just nod and go home
To my TV
To my flickering computer screen
To my silent scream

The bigger and balder your lies
The more I cover my eyes
The more I applaud
The more of your drugs I take to keep me
anesthetised
If you want you can cut off my balls

Don't ask me what I think because I don't
You can do that for me
You tell me
Because I don't know
Please tell me what to do and say
I'll even kill my neighbours and family if you
want me to
Shall I?

The world's gone mad hasn't it?
Kill old people and take their money
Go to jail for standing for freedom
Get rewarded for genocide
Pay through the nose for sanitation
Spy on your neighbours
Promote de-motivation

The world's gone upside down
All things real are demonised
All things demon are lionised
Nothing makes sense
The world's gone mental
Fights its wars in the temple
Kills the planet
Kills the gods
And replaces them with a limited edition
Boyzone CD box-set with holographic cover
and free temporary tattoo

Thousand Yard Stare

I've blown a fuse
I've been silenced by the world's workings
I've wept myself to sleep

I've just been trying to live as quietly and humbly
as I can
And yet a large nut has appeared in my head
This dark
Heavy
Constricting mass keeps my thoughts earthbound

Something has caused a serious shutdown
Something has clipped the wings of my thought
processes
Something keeps me in sadness

It is the seizure of the left side of my brain
Brought about by the improbability of logic
It is frustration with numbers beyond compare
It is self preservation
But I beseech the universe

Please bring back my imagination

Self Sabotage

We walk the tight-wire of exquisite existence
Counting each new near topple-swoon to take our
gift
Earthbound ringmaster orchestrate the boos
Scupper our clown's mast ladder accent

The Masters of Muddle

The masters of muddle
Waddle in a puddle of muddle

The masters of muddle
Fiddle in the middle of a fuddling trouble

The masters of muddle
Fiddle-faddle in a bundle of fuddle

The masters of muddle
Paddle while addled
They piddle while raddled in rubble

Quiet Street

Life's so neat and ordered
Divided into boxes
I'm living in a geometry
Where everything is spotless

Stripe the lawn and clean the car
I'll ask the wife to sweep the path
Watch out ants and plughole hair
Watch out dirt you'd better not dare

We're spick and span and shipshape
And jolly spot on too
We're spick and span and shipshape
Come on let's scrub the loo

If something comes to ruffle me
I'll be on it straight away
So that I can live tomorrow the way I lived
today

The Master Race Wears Sunglasses

Tattoos and piercings are mainstream
A "Che" or red star on your shirt don't mean a
thing
It don't matter if you're poor or rich
Or nice or a bitch
I am not fooled by dreadlocks
Or mohicans or sandals
I know it's a scandal
Just one more status symbol
Bought by another asinine arse in a four wheel
drive
As another species dies
To fuel our lust for vanity
Profanity or lack of sanity

Gypsy Ska
Tekno Ragga
Industrial Leftfield are all in the charts
Luvvies are lovers of Post-Punk-Garage
Dummies and posers groove to the latest new
tune the papers tell us is over the moon

Buy your revolution from the façade of fairness
Buy your freedom from empty equality
Don't be a killjoy
Don't be static
Bolt on your green revolution
Buy a couple of kilos of save the planet recycled
plastic

I think you look beautiful as you admire your life
in the mirror
Just answer me this
Why is your mouth so miserable and your eyes so
full of terror?

Uniform of Sadness

Black shirt
Long black shorts
Black cap
Skull and bones on your back

Marching to the tune of black
Marching to the tune of sadness
Devoid of any colour
Devoid of any gladness

Tats up your arms
Pins through your skin
Tats up your arms
Suffering regime

Blind leading blind
Down a black ally
Body armour's not your friend
Your heart's your only ally

Baggy
Chains hanging down
Looking like a clown
In bondage to a look
But the world don't give a fuck

Suicide sorrow misery
Clones are never free
Shine don't be a fool
Forget about their rules

Graffiti by an anonymous artist (original in colour)

Sucking Satan's Cock

A blood curdling scream
A sickening nauseous shock
As I am surgically removed from sleep

My inner policeman puppeteer dresses me
And walks my ghost around the house

I brace myself
And then walk through the "Stars 'round their
heads" curtain
To take on the world and his wife

I start to breathe his foul stench
I start to kick against his shit with my rising
anger

Another zombie day
I'm sucking fucking Satan's cock

Clock my corpse in
Clock my mind out
Lost souls around me
Scream and shout

My ears are filling up with metal
This is the source of hatred eternal

After all my commitments
I have only a few pennies
Don't call me crazy
Just call me a lemming

I'm sucking fucking Satan's cock

Everyday Man

Blocking out feeling
Laughing to diffuse the pain
Confused and ignorant
Passing the blame

Looking for allies
To justify cruelty
Sharing banality
Not living reality

Lined up lemmings
Lobotomised drones
Wound up to work the machine
Human (but) not being

Souls hiding in hardness
Every day brings a sharpness
A sickening waste
An overripe nauseous taste

Each grin
Forced smile
Each child defiled
Every penny has an added weight
Every action another added mile

Taking us to sadness

Suicide Note

Part 1

Something frightening is able to rise up in me
now
Something that demands we all take notice
Screaming
Shouting
Crying
Shaking
Something that's ready to kill whatever dares to
try and stop it

A child out of control
A child which thinks nothing can stop it
A child which will go all the way
And then kill itself to make the mess and hurt
disappear

Part 2

I am so sad
I must be having some sort of breakdown

I can no longer work
I try but just break down in tears
Or shake
Drool and jabber like a loon

My usefulness seems to be over
I don't feel valued by anyone or anything

My self esteem is rock bottom
What's left for me now?

My credit is literally and metaphorically all
used up
I've reached the end of the line
The game's up

Part 3

No
I'm not alright

Graffiti by an anonymous artist (original in colour)

Unconsciousness

Treading a thin crust
Treading a dry thin crust of glass
Maybe I'll slip
Crack
Fall

Unconsciousness...

Safety Nazis

Metros and caravans
Volvos and campervans
Tractors and milk floats
Grannies and cunts in suits

Families and tourists
Builders that are pissed
Police cars and funeral stuff
Train-spotters with eyes full of fluff

Lorries that belch out smoke
Teenagers smoking dope
Old cars that are broke
Villages with carnival floats

Trailers with piles of hay
Gipsy horses pulling a dray
Queues and queues of drones
Businessmen on mobile phones

Buses taking kids to school
Motorcycles acting the fool
Green "L's" you're in my way
Go on punks make my day

Traction engines and wide loads
Escaped ducks sheep or toads
Dustbin men doing a deal
You're asleep at the fucking wheel

Fuck you all
Fuck you all
Because I want to get past
Don't slow me down you safety Nazis
Don't slow me down
Don't flash my number
Don't threaten me

Dogs and Cats

Have you trodden in anything lately?

Fucking dogs and fucking cats
They fucking piss
They fucking crap
They fucking stink
They fucking cost
Why don't they all get fucking lost?

They fucking whine
They fucking cry
They fucking bark
Don't ask me why

Fucking cats kill little fucking birds
Fucking dogs eat each other's fucking turds
They suck up to their fucking owners
So they don't end up fucking homeless

With their sycophantic fawning whimpers
They'll have you bending over fucking
backwards
Catty nibbles doggy treats
I'd give them fuck all to eat

They fucking scratch
They fucking bite
Cats and dogs are fucking shite!

Pervert's Poem

I have got to fuck you up the bum
On your toes I'd like to cum
I want to piss into your hair
And while you spank me hear you swear

Tickle my testicles with a feather
Wrap my cock in patent leather
Rub my nipples with chilli oil
Put clothes pegs on my balls

I want to dress up as a tart
Have my tongue pierced while you light my
farts
I must have a group sex scene
Or even appear in a magazine

I want fun while in a lift
I want fun while smoking spliffs
I want sex out of doors
I want fetish
More
More
More

Bristol Club

Low fuzz-drone
Mind-buzzed
Bomb-bass
White-noise
Temperature confusion
Dark
Fizzing
Voidoid death

Club
Pub
Puke
Fuck
Dumb
Funk
Loud and lost

Hide and hold
Beer looking queer
Where to go?
Sweating
Fretting
Shitting

Empty
Blind
Stark
Drunk
Sunken
Paranoid drug shiver
Blurred
Loud

Wet
Dirty girl
Flirty creep
Skin
Glow
Peep
Smell
Sticky

F
a
l
l

The Information Age

I'm living in the information age
I can be half or twice my age
I can talk to everybody in the world
I can watch everything as it unfurls

I can see what hasn't happened
I can hear what hasn't been
I know
I'll invent something weird
I'll see what my mum looks like with a beard

Yesterday?
Forget it mate
I want it now before it's too late
If I move real quick I'll make some money
So I better start hopping like the Easter bunny

Who are you?
You're not real
I don't exist either
And I can't really feel

I know I'll change my name
Eat food delivered by laser beam
Have I been here before?
It seems the same

Oh shit!
I'm stuck to this flickering screen
Millions of Munch's letting out a scream
Billions of minds unable to dream

75   *Richard Allen*

Kaki-Land

Sweet gold and ruby jewels
Hang suspended in the naked trees
But the orchard lies beyond high walls
Guarded by seven sly masked beasts

The first gnawed my bones with a deathly haw
The second cruelly tricked me
I followed to a cliff edge fall
The third hid itself betwixt my ears
That I might doubt myself and fear
The fourth and fifth both sold me out
One to laugh and burst his belt
The other to abuse and at me shout
Being not like him
The sixth he ripped me from my skin
Scarred and bitter
I need the winter sun upon my lips
I pray the seventh show me tenderness

King of the Hoodies

King of the hoodies
Eleven months behind bars
King of the hoodies
Now it's December he's 'avin' it large

He's a paedophile
He's a knifeman
He's a paedophile
He's not a nice man

He'll bounce you on his knee
But he'll have his cock right up your arse
He'll steal all of your money
What a fucking farce

King of the hoodies
Without question he's the chief
Where did he get his goodies?
I'll tell you
He's a bloody thief!

Be careful of this guy
He's in your neighbourhood
Stealing peoples' lives
From under his red hood

Mouth-Breather

Mouth-breather
You bastard
Where do you come from?
To sneak up on me in the night and tie a little
knot in my stomach

Nu Metal

All persons belonging
Vulgar shit
A nation race
Defecate
Tribe
Get rid of excrement
Community faeces
Warlike people
English speaking act of defecation
Get rid of persons in general
Nonsense persons belonging to a place
Despicable
Forming a company or class expressing anger
Having rank
Anonymous position

Ego Kills

I'm living on an island of my own design
I've got no friends to speak of
Because I'm just not trying
I've tried to find a job
But no one wants to know
I think myself an artist
In truth I do fuck all

You not in denial like me
Real woman you're free
You're not from an alien race
And I think that you'll agree
That now I feel so humble
Because I've started to think
I've looked real close at my little life
And accept some things just stink

Ego kills my love
Ego kills my friends
Ego stops me growing
It stops my life from flowing

I'm boiling in my body-bag
Come and pierce my skin
I cut you all my real bad looks
But you just won't give in
Even when you're up on hooks
And I block you with my body
Or when you're calm and gentle
My ego tells me "Enemy!"

Part IV

I Revolt

When my enemies arrive, they will discover that I have their hats on the end of my sword

Turn It Over

Turn a table over
Do your arms a favour
Turn a tune too loud
Do your I a rainbow

Turn your words right over
Free your wrongs from underneath a maybe

Look at all the corners
Get off your straight line ride
Queue for no one and no lies
Don't be blinded by could bes or your bloody
pride

Just turn it over
Turn a table over

Graffiti by an anonymous artist (original in colour)

Just Words

It's just words
Only words
If it's words it don't matter
If it's flowers or guns
It's all just couplets
And rhyming
And puns
You know it makes sense
This free styling fun
Because we can put hate
And fear on the run
Bullets for vowels
Armamentation for punctuation
To shoot down bigotry
And ego inflation

World Domination and War
(This Is the Time for a Changing)

You said it was all said back then
You said it was all sung back when
We were young and naïve
Hippies and Beats
But it's not true
Is it?

So we're all grown up now
Don't have long hair
Smoke dope or wear flowers
So it's all OK now
Is it?

To blow up homes mums and kids
A train road factory or bridge
So you take control
Of car sales and phones
Of Caribbean bananas
Chocolate milkshake and trousers
Of beer pizza and ciggies
Which are sold to young kiddies
So they are your slaves from cradle to grave

Bob Dylan's long gone
We are not freaks
You've been found out
We'll continue to shout
This is the time for a changing
Isn't it?

Ultimate Rock

Leather-clad speed-freak poppin' suicide pills
It's Rock 'n' Roll baby
Born to kill

Guitar-biker-shaman on a death-wish mission
Turn up the volume
Hardcore nuclear fission

Jailbreak candy-girl gimmy my fill
Blow me into orbit baby
I'm addicted to thrills

Tribal outlaw
Revolution burning
Crank out the real deal
Where's your yearning?

Space clone invasion
No way out
Psychotic apocalypse
Scream and shout

Metal nutter's war-cry
Zombie rock strut
Dynamite 'n' trippin' out
I don't give a fuck

Ultimate Rock baby
Ultimate Rock
Harder than Rock baby
Harder than Rock
Ultimate
Ultimate
Ultimate
Rock

Stop the Bloody Warring

Stop the bloody warring
Stop the bloody bombing
Stop the helpless losing
Stop the empty winning
Stop the bloody shooting
Stop the bloody maiming
Stop the bloody killing

Stop the bloody warring
Stop the pimping
Stop the whoring
Stop the bloody robbing
Stop the cheating
The taking
The hunger
The thirst and the greed
Stop and think about our children's needs

Stop the bloody warring

If All the World Were Coppers

If all the world were coppers
If all the world were pigs
If all the world were coppers
Would we all be bloody nicked?

If all the world were coppers
Would we all be good as gold?
If all the world were coppers
Would we do what we're told?

If we were all the goodies
Where would we find the baddies?
If we were all the law
Who'd knock on our door?

Bollocks to the coppers
Bollocks to the Queen
Bollocks to the Church
And any uniforms I see

Bollocks to the government
Whether blue or red
Bollocks to the system
I'll use what's in my head

If all our homes were prisons
Where would we all go?
To escape the spies and illusions
To decide who's friend or foe?

If all our homes were prisons
Would we drug ourselves with TV?
Or would we rise up from our sofas
Open our eyes and see?

If all our homes were prisons
Would we all stay inside?
Or would we seek liaisons
With those on the outside?

Bollocks to the prisons
Bollocks to the walls
Let's all hold a vision
To break down barriers

Bollocks to the Nazis
And wherever they may hide
Bollocks to the silence
That keeps them in their stride

If all our streets were empty
Would we try and take them back
A conveyor belt of coffins
Overpriced and over taxed

If all our streets were curfewed
Would we all tow the line?
Or would we say
"It's for the best, they keep us safe and that's
just fine."?

If all our streets were cold
Without a tree in sight
Would we take a shovel
To bring earth and warmth and light?

Bollocks to destruction of our neighbourhoods
Bollocks to pollution of our sea and sky and
woods
Bollocks to the thieves who run this fucking con
Bollocks to their cronies
Let's put them on the run

Bollocks to these verses
Bollocks to this rhyme
In case you've all forgotten
I'll say it one more time

Bollocks to the government
Whether blue or red
Bollocks to the system
I'll use what's in my head

Motor-Mouth

I've lit the blue touch paper
So stand well back
I'm gonna start talkin'
'Till I have a heart attack

Let my tongue flap about like an outboard
motor
Whip it up into a frenzy like a helicopter rotor
Bring out the alphabet for all to see
Paint people's ears 'till they can't breath

Lips are moving like oceans
Teeth flying out are part of the potion
I'm headed on in to an electrical system
I'm sat on a turbo charged racing car piston

Never givin' up 'cause I'm a trier
Never givin' up 'cause I'm no liar
Never givin' up 'till my brain catches fire
Never givin' up 'till I'm on a funeral pyre

Peas

We're in our garden from dawn to dusk
Growing things that we can trust
Organic veg for us to eat
Good and tasty
Hard to beat

You won't catch us pushing supermarket
trolleys
Filled up with giant corn that's not so jolly
We want to see a bit of mud
Not this phoney
Coloured
Plastic crud

Our stuff ain't sprayed with synthetic goo
It's not been sized or polished
Or called class one food
And it sure as hell ain't made in a test tube

We're growing peas
We're growing peas
We're growing peas

So go out to a local plot
Drop in some seeds and watch them sprout up
It ain't that tough
It ain't that hard
That's why God gave us all a back yard

Hill and Tree

Hey!
Where's our hill gone?
They took it over there to build a road
Greedy toads
Hey!
Where's our tree gone?
It was in the way
So they chopped it up and put it in the bin
What a sin
Thoughtless folks
What a joke

I liked our hill
Now it's just a scar
Will they fill it in?
Why didn't they ask us?
Maybe they did
But we didn't hear so they assumed we'd shed
no tears
They just took it over there
Squashed it flat and that was that

Did they ask me about the tree?
I wouldn't let it go for free
What do you mean "No"?
I'm going to write to the papers
Or go on a TV show
But that's not my style
So I'll wait a while
And in the place where it grew
Grow two

For Erik, Star and the Others

You brought me the air
To utter the chants
You brought me the fire
To relight a passion
You brought me the water
To heal my compassion
You brought me the earth
To ground my expression
You brought me the spirit
To find my earth family
You brought me the centre
To help me find me

You gave me two weeks
To nail my shit down
You gave me a course
To grow green from the brown

I hope in my turn I can "fix (the) shit up"
Even if it means taking crap from the cops

From the scunge
And the grunge
And the minge
And the mange
Together we'll throw
And sow a million seed-balls of change

The Dreamer (Getting Up)

Someone's soaked my skin in glue
And filled my skull with clay
Overnight I've been stuck to the bed
I am paralyzed by electrostatic microwaves

But hope can help me struggle free
That ambition can flower and change
Can I ever doubt my vital dreams?
Be languishing with the living dead?
Broken into many parts and scattered over fields?

So I arise and shake my aching bones
Bring water to the desert of my mouth and nose
And eyes
And ears
And hands
And throat
Let life return and the garden of creativity start to
sprout

Now I've returned to this world
There is only one thing to do
Take up my paper
Take up my pen
And carry Bob Dylan's baton through
The fascists and their friends
Through the thieves
The greedy and the murderers
To idealism at the end

Doom-Monger 1

Doom-monger
May your tongue turn blue and fall from your
mouth
Stop your froth
Just turn it off!

All the leaders know full well there's no real
risk
They know what we resist persists
It's all just a game
To get us down to that golf sale
So we can take comfort
Feel good and feel cool
Keep on smiling
Keep on buying
Keep on lying to ourselves
So we keep on emptying the supermarket
shelves

Doom-monger
Don't be a bore
You know we're living in post-democracy
After all you voted for it
Remember you're free!
We all know the score
Information's waiting at the station
We just need a revolution
To revolve the revelation
So we can forget our pain
And step on the train

Doom-Monger 2

I just met a friend on the street
She said the US and China have a beef
Maybe the president has a problem with his
Chinese
Difficulties with culture and language sure don't
help with good understandage

Well they've run through the Middle East for
fun
Next they'll nuke Iran
I've heard there's a murmur something will
happen in Burma
They say soon there'll be no more commies
Dictators or terrorists
The world will be off the hook
We'll all be safe in our beds
Tucked up with a good book

But I said
Hey wait a minute
Have you been to China?
Are they all loading their guns?
Were you in Al-Qaeda?
Are they all on the run?

Then I said
I haven't a telly
I like to go out in the rain in my wellies
So let the papers pile high on street corners
While I watch the leaves fall this autumn

Richard Allen

"City on Fire" acrylic paint on paper by the author
(original in colour)

A Humble Grumble

A sea of faces flash past
Each one a wave of lines
Tension
Each one a monotonous monologue of
frustration
Be still
Hold your tongues
You strike a familiar tone of dissatisfaction
You are all on a conveyor belt of conversation
Unable to
Or too lazy to get off

Shout out loud with actions
Shout out with every nerve
Shake the foundations of what you dislike
Shake them with your bare hands

If you don't jam the flow of apathy
You will be carried by its current
To a place where every record is scratched
And every pencil needs sharpening

Forgive

Benevolent smile
Respectful gazes
Reverent approach
Your office has instant wise man appeal
I'm not knocking it
Good luck to you
Because it seems to me a burden to bear

But I'm not a hero worshipper
I'm not a stationary boy
I'm a big fan of no guru
No office
No pips
No stripes
No egg
No medals
No rank
No uniform
No colour
Because we are all priests to one another
(If only we could realise)

So have faith in your brothers
Share soul with your sisters
Allow good things to happen
Unfold your aura
Your body
Your dreams
Open up your heart
Forgive one another
Forgive your lovers
Forgive your family
Your neighbours and all others
And play your part

How Much Longer?

I've been listening to Dylan
He sure had it nailed
And there are others too
Who tell it how it is
Tell a truthful tale

How much longer can we walk on down the
street
As our neighbour's being battered
While lying at our feet?

How much longer can we ride on down the road
While thieves are taking our children's minds
On the battlefield of food?

We're living in the information age
We all know what's going on
There are no excuses any more for tolerating
injustices
For pretending we do no wrongs

So don't look the other way
Whistle and roll your eyes
A big brain's not needed to predict their
surprises and lies
Use your money
Your body
Your voice
Make protest your issue
Your song of choice

INDEX OF POEMS

Lightning Source UK Ltd.
Milton Keynes UK
UKOW04f0011291013

219967UK00001B/20/P